Spectacular
Animal Towns

The Prairie Dog's Town
A Perfect Hideaway

by Miriam Aronin

Consultants: Joy Gober and Pete Gober,
Biologists at the U.S. Fish & Wildlife Service

BEARPORT
PUBLISHING

New York, New York

Credits

Cover and Title Page, © Steven Dijkman/iStockphoto, nhtg/Shutterstock, and Mariusz S. Jurgielewicz/Shutterstock; TOC, © Kevin L Chesson/Shutterstock; 4, © Juniors Bildarchiv/Alamy; 5, © Jim Brandenburg/Minden Pictures; 6, © Jim Brandenburg/Minden Pictures; 7, © Henk Bentlage/Shutterstock; 8, © W. Perry Conway/Corbis; 10, © laozein/Alamy; 11, © Jaana Piira/Shutterstock; 12, © D. Robert & Lorri Franz/Corbis; 13, © Jeff Vanuga/Nature Picture Library; 14, © Bruce Coleman USA/Photoshot; 15, © Mila Zinkova; 16, © C.Huetter/Arco Images/Alamy; 17, © Kevin Schafer/Corbis; 18, © H. Reinhard/Arco Images/Alamy; 19, © Karel Gallas/Shuttersttock; 20, © Jim Brandenburg/Minden Pictures; 21, © W. Perry Conway/Corbis; 22, © Gordon & Cathy Illg/Animals Animals Enterprises; 23, © George D. Lepp/Corbis; 25, © photazz/Shutterstock; 26L, © Pat Caulfield/PhotoResearchers, Inc.; 26R, © Rod Planck/NHPA/Photoshot; 27, © LaNae Christenson/Shutterstock; 28, © Dave Massey/Shutterstock; 29T, © Rick & Nora Bowers/Alamy; 29B, © H. Reinhard/Arco Images/Alamy; 32, © David Dohnal/Shutterstock.

Publisher: Kenn Goin
Senior Editor: Lisa Wiseman
Creative Director: Spencer Brinker
Design: Dawn Beard Creative
Photo Researcher: Picture Perfect Professionals, LLC

Library of Congress Cataloging-in-Publication Data

Aronin, Miriam.
  The prairie dog's town : a perfect hideaway / by Miriam Aronin.
    p. cm. — (Spectacular animal towns)
  Includes bibliographical references and index.
  ISBN-13: 978-1-59716-870-0 (library binding)
  ISBN-10: 1-59716-870-X (library binding)
  1. Prairie dogs—Habitations—Juvenile literature. I. Title.

QL737.R68A77 2010
599.36'7—dc22

                    2009004064

Copyright © 2010 Bearport Publishing Company, Inc. All rights reserved. No part of this publication may be reproduced in whole or in part, stored in a retrieval system, or transmitted in any form or by any means, electronic, mechanical, photocopying, recording, or otherwise, without written permission from the publisher.

For more information, write to Bearport Publishing Company, Inc., 101 Fifth Avenue, Suite 6R, New York, New York 10003. Printed in the United States of America.

10 9 8 7 6 5 4 3 2 1

Contents

A Tremendous Town

In 1902, **biologist** Vernon Bailey traveled to Texas so that he could study the animals that lived there. In some areas, Vernon saw small furry creatures almost everywhere. They were "standing at the entrances to their holes, flipping their tails, and steadily barking."

A prairie dog is not really a dog. It's a kind of squirrel. It got its name from the barking sounds it makes.

What were these small animals? They were black-tailed **prairie dogs**. The holes they stood next to led to underground homes called **burrows**. Vernon **estimated** that these burrows made up a huge town of about 400 million prairie dogs.

The prairie dog town that Vernon found covered 16 million acres (6.5 million hectares). That is bigger than the state of West Virginia. In fact, it is the largest prairie dog town ever discovered by humans!

Prairie dogs live on grassy lands called prairies, which are mostly located in the west-central United States. They share the prairies with many other animals, such as bison.

Black-tailed prairie dogs are the most common **species** of prairie dog. The other types are the Mexican prairie dog, the Gunnison's prairie dog, the white-tailed prairie dog, and the Utah prairie dog.

Family Life in a Town

Today prairie dog towns are much smaller than the one that Vernon Bailey found. Towns usually cover less than 100 acres (40.5 hectares)—about the area of 75 football fields.

A prairie dog town

Prairie dog towns are similar to human towns because family members live together. However, prairie dog families, called **coteries**, are different than human families. Their families usually include one adult male, a few adult females, and their young. The members of each family work together to dig their burrows.

Each coterie has anywhere from 5 to as many as 35 family members.

A prairie dog town is made up of many families that may or may not be related. Each family, however, lives in its own home area or **territory**.

Deep Burrows

Each coterie may have several burrows within its territory. Burrows keep prairie dogs safe from most **predators**, such as hawks and coyotes. These animals are too big to follow prairie dogs down into their underground homes.

Burrows also keep prairie dogs safe from harsh weather. The deep holes stay cool in summer and warm in winter.

This coyote cannot reach the prairie dogs inside this burrow.

Like human homes, prairie dog burrows have many rooms, known as **chambers**, that are used in different ways. For example, some rooms are used for sleeping, while others, called **nurseries**, are where prairie dogs raise their young. There are even special chambers used as restrooms, where prairie dogs store their wastes.

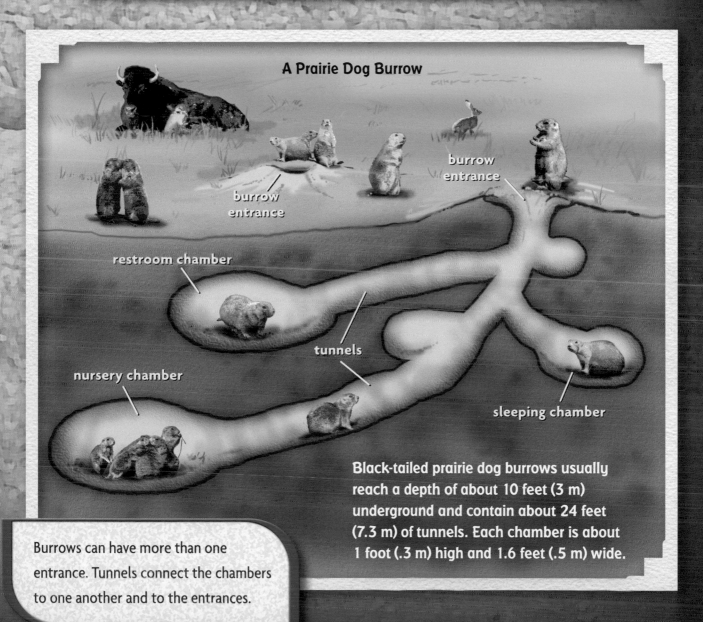

A Prairie Dog Burrow

burrow entrance

burrow entrance

restroom chamber

tunnels

nursery chamber

sleeping chamber

Black-tailed prairie dog burrows usually reach a depth of about 10 feet (3 m) underground and contain about 24 feet (7.3 m) of tunnels. Each chamber is about 1 foot (.3 m) high and 1.6 feet (.5 m) wide.

Burrows can have more than one entrance. Tunnels connect the chambers to one another and to the entrances.

Mound Builders

Prairie dogs make burrows by digging in the dirt with their claws. As they dig, they pile up dirt in a **mound** around the burrow entrance. Some mounds are more than two feet (.6 m) high.

A burrow entrance with a rim crater

There are two different types of mounds. Burrow openings with low, wide, loosely shaped mounds are called dome craters. Other burrow entrances that have higher, carefully shaped mounds that look like tiny volcanoes are called rim craters.

Prairie dogs build mounds for many reasons. For example, they prevent flooding by blocking rainwater that could pour into the burrow from the surrounding land. Mounds also help prairie dogs breathe underground. Some burrows have both a high and a low entrance. Air comes into the burrow at the low entrance. As the air becomes warm, it rises and moves toward the higher entrance. This keeps air flowing throughout the burrow.

A burrow opening with a dome crater

Sounding the Alarm

Prairie dogs often stand on top of a mound to spot predators. Each adult takes turns keeping watch. As soon as an enemy is spotted, the guard "sounds the alarm" by letting out a high-pitched barking sound. Prairie dogs that hear the noise know it's not safe to be outside.

Both male and female prairie dogs sound the alarm when predators get too close.

Some scientists believe prairie dogs can change their alarm calls to share more information about nearby danger. For example, an alarm call might tell whether a predator is in the air or on the ground, and how quickly the enemy is moving.

As the other prairie dogs rush to their burrows, their voices join the alarm call. The warning spreads quickly to more prairie dogs in the town. It gives them a chance to escape to safety in their underground homes.

A few predators, such as black-footed ferrets, can invade a prairie dog burrow. If prairie dogs can escape outside, they may use dirt to close the burrow's entrance and trap the predator underground.

Prairie Dog Communication

Besides their high-pitched barking, prairie dogs have others ways to **communicate**. For example, black-tailed prairie dogs make "jump-yip" calls, which signal that danger has passed.

To make this call, a prairie dog stands on its back feet. Then it throws its front feet in the air and calls out. Once a prairie dog starts the signal, other town members will pass it on.

Some scientists say that the "jump-yip" call sounds like a sneeze.

Coterie members also greet one another in a special way—they touch teeth. It looks like the prairie dogs are kissing.

Families are less friendly to prairie dogs outside their coteries, however. They will fight any stranger that enters their territory.

As many as six prairie dogs may "kiss" at the same time.

When prairie dogs fight, they chatter their teeth, raise their tails, and make barking noises. Two prairie dogs may chase each other and fight for as long as half an hour. They may get hurt but do not usually kill each other.

Summer Days in Town

During the summer, it's especially important for prairie dogs to be able to quickly warn each other of danger. Why? When the weather is warm, the little animals spend most of their time outside **foraging** for food such as leaves, grasses, and seeds. This makes it very easy for aboveground predators to hunt and kill them.

A prairie dog eating

In warm weather, prairie dogs spend more than 95 percent of the day outside.

Summer is also when coterie members spend a lot of time together. They dig burrows and protect their territory as a family. They also play with and **groom** one another.

When coterie members groom one another, they remove insects and clean each other's fur.

Ready for Winter

During the fall, the animals get ready for winter. They eat extra food because their favorite meals will be **scarce** during the cold months. They store this food as fat in their bodies.

Extra fat helps black-tailed prairie dogs survive the winter.

Different kinds of prairie dogs handle the winter in different ways. For example, on cold snowy days, black-tailed prairie dogs stay in their burrows and sleep. They get energy from their fat, which lets them go several days without food. Then on sunny winter days, they leave their burrows to warm up in the sunshine. They also forage for foods such as plant roots.

Gunnison's, white-tailed, and Utah prairie dogs spend their winters very differently. They are **inactive**. From November to March, they **hibernate** in their burrows.

Prairie dogs that don't hibernate forage for food throughout the winter.

Up to 14 black-tailed prairie dogs may sleep in one burrow during the cold winter months.

Babies in the Burrow

When winter ends, prairie dogs become more active. By March or April, adult females **mate** with the male in their coterie.

The day after mating, each pregnant female chooses a chamber for her nursery. There, she builds a grassy nest. She does not let any other adults enter the nursery.

A pregnant female moves dry grass that she will use to make a nest in her nursery.

After about a month, the female gives birth to between two and eight babies, called pups. The pups stay in the burrow for six weeks. During this time, their mother makes milk to feed them.

Five-week-old black-tailed prairie dogs sleep inside a burrow.

Prairie dog pups are born with no hair and with their eyes shut. They weigh about half an ounce (14 g)— less than the weight of three nickels.

The Town Grows

Young prairie dogs in a coterie are brothers and sisters. They have the same father and sometimes the same mother. To find a mate from a different family, young prairie dogs must travel to a new area. They will leave their parents' coterie when they are about one year old to start their own families.

Pups stay with their mother's coterie for at least one year.

Many young prairie dogs form new coteries at the edge of their town. They move into unused burrows or dig new ones. As more prairie dogs move to the edge of a town, the town grows.

Young prairie dogs playing

Sometimes adult prairie dogs **relocate** to the edge of a town because there is more food to be found in these less **populated** areas.

Towns in Danger

Around 200 years ago, about one billion prairie dogs lived in North America. Since then, the prairie dog population has dropped by 98 percent. What happened?

Beginning in the early 1900s, some **ranchers** feared that hungry prairie dogs would not leave enough grass for their cattle. So they decided to get rid of the small animals by poisoning them.

Prairie Dogs in the Wild

☐ Where prairie dogs live

Prairie dogs live mainly in the west-central United States.

Another problem prairie dogs have faced over the years is **habitat** destruction. People have plowed up prairies for farmland or have covered the prairies with human cities and towns, leaving these animals with no place to live.

Prairie dogs have also faced a deadly disease called **sylvatic plague**. Most prairie dogs that catch it die. This disease, which spreads quickly in large prairie dog groups, can wipe out entire towns.

Cattle and prairie dogs both eat wild prairie grasses.

Sylvatic plague is spread by fleas that live on prairie dogs and other wild animals. In very rare cases, it spreads to humans. When this happens, it's called bubonic (byoo-BOHN-ic) plague.

Protecting Prairie Dog Towns

It is important to save prairie dogs from disease and human threats. Why? The animals play a large role in the prairie **ecosystem**. For example, animals such as black-footed ferrets, badgers, and eagles need prairie dogs for food. Without them, some of these animals would die out and others would have to work much harder to find food.

ATTENTION
BLACK-FOOTED FERRET REINTRODUCTION AREA
The Forest Service, in cooperation with National Park Service, Fish & Wildlife Service and SD Game, Fish & Parks are reintroducing the endangered black-footed ferret to this area. Pursuant to the Endangered Species Act, the Forest Service is prohibiting prairie dog hunting/shooting in this area. Please contact the Forest Service office in Wall for further information (605) 279-2125.
PRAIRIE DOG
HUNTING / SHOOTING
PROHIBITED

Attention!

Scientists studying prairie dogs mark the animals to keep better track of their activities.

Animals such as burrowing owls also need prairie dogs. They use the empty burrows for their homes.

It is now against the law to hurt or kill Mexican and Utah prairie dogs. Many people are working to protect black-tailed prairie dogs, too.

Scientists are also testing a **vaccine** to protect prairie dogs from sylvatic plague. They hope these efforts will help keep prairie dogs safe and allow them to keep building their spectacular underground towns for many years to come.

Prairie Dog Town Facts

Prairie dogs are small animals related to squirrels. They live in family groups called coteries, which are part of larger groups called towns. Here are some more facts about prairie dogs and their amazing towns.

Length	12–18 inches (30.5–46 cm) long, including the tail
Weight	2–4 pounds (.9–1.8 kg)
Fur Color	yellowish or reddish
Food	grasses, leaves, and seeds; in the winter, plant roots and stems
Town Size	usually between one acre and several thousand acres (.4 hectares and several hundred hectares), but most often less than 100 acres (40.5 hectares)
Town Population	historically from 5 prairie dogs up to several million prairie dogs; today the number is much less
Habitat	mainly in the grassy prairies of the west-central United States; also found in parts of southern Canada and northern Mexico
Life Span	3 to 4 years in the wild

More Animal Towns

Prairie dogs are not the only animals that work together to build spectacular animal towns. Here are two others.

Muskrats
- Muskrats are small, furry animals that live in wet areas, such as marshes, in North America.
- Muskrats build nests by piling water plants onto a solid base, such as a tree stump.
- They also dig burrows at the edges of bodies of water. The animals can enter their burrows from underwater.
- The members of a muskrat family group share one nest or burrow. During winter, they live together in one chamber to stay warm.
- Muskrat families live in territories about 200 feet (61 m) across.

Beavers
- Beavers are medium-size furry animals that live in watery areas in North America, Europe, and Asia.
- Beavers build their homes, or lodges, out of tree branches and mud.
- Lodges are often located in the middle of ponds and look like small islands.
- Beavers live in family groups. Families include an adult male, an adult female, and their young.

Glossary

biologist (bye-OL-uh-jist) a scientist who studies plants or animals

burrows (BUR-ohz) tunnels or holes in the ground made by some animals for shelter

chambers (CHAYM-burz) separate rooms found in prairie dog burrows

communicate (kuh-MYOO-nuh-kate) to share information

coteries (KOH-tuh-reez) families of prairie dogs

ecosystem (EE-koh-*siss*-tuhm) a community of plants and animals that depend on one another to live

estimated (ESS-ti-*mate*-id) to have figured out the approximate amount of something

foraging (FOR-ij-ing) looking for food in the wild

groom (GROOM) to clean

habitat (HAB-uh-*tat*) a place in nature where plants or animals normally live

hibernate (HYE-bur-nate) to go into a sleeplike state during periods of cold weather

inactive (in-AK-tiv) not doing anything; not active

mate (MATE) to come together to have young

mound (MOUND) a small hill or pile of dirt

nurseries (NUR-sur-eez) places set aside for babies or young animals

populated (POP-yuh-lay-tid) an area that has animals or people living there

prairie dogs (PRAIR-ee DAWGZ) small burrowing mammals found mainly in the plains of west-central North America

predators (PRED-uh-turz) animals that hunt and kill other animals for food

ranchers (RAN-churz) people who own or manage ranches

relocate (ri-LOH-kate) to find another place to live

scarce (SKAIRSS) hard to find

species (SPEE-sheez) groups that animals are divided into, according to similar characteristics; members of the same species can have offspring together

sylvatic plague (sil-VAT-ik PLAYG) a disease that is transmitted by fleas and affects many species of wild rodents

territory (TER-uh-*tor*-ee) a region or an area of land that belongs to an animal

vaccine (vak-SEEN) medicine that protects a person or animal from a particular disease

Bibliography

Doughty, Robin W. "Prairie Dog." *The Handbook of Texas Online.*
www.tshaonline.org/handbook/online/articles/PP/tcp1.html

Hoogland, John L., ed. *Conservation of the Black-Tailed Prairie Dog: Saving North America's Western Grasslands.* Washington, D.C.: Island Press (2006).

Johnsgard, Paul A. *Prairie Dog Empire: A Saga of the Shortgrass Prairie.* Lincoln, NE: University of Nebraska Press (2005).

May, Holly L. "Black-tailed Prairie Dog (*Cynomis ludovicianis*)," *Natural Resources Conservation Service, Wildlife Habitat Management Institute,* No. 23 (January 2003). **ftp://ftp-fc.sc.egov.usda.gov/WHMI/WEB/pdf/Prairie_dog.pdf**

Read More

Mader, Jan. *Living on a Prairie.* New York: Children's Press (2004).

Markle, Sandra. *Prairie Dogs: Animal Prey.* Minneapolis, MN: Lerner Publications Company (2007).

Patent, Dorothy Hinshaw. *Prairie Dogs.* New York: Clarion Books (1993).

Learn More Online

To learn more about prairie dogs and their towns, visit
www.bearportpublishing.com/SpectacularAnimalTowns

Index

About the Author

Miriam Aronin is a writer and editor. She enjoys reading, knitting, and visiting animals at the zoo.

WITHDRAWN

DATE DUE

The Columbus Academy
Reinberger Middle School Library
4300 Cherry Bottom Road
Gahanna, Ohio 43230